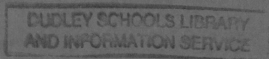
KU-453-181

AMAZING JOURNEYS

Down a River

Carole Telford and Rod Theodorou

www.heinemann.co.uk/library
Visit our website to find out more information about Heinemann Library books.

To order:
☎ Phone 44 (0) 1865 888112
🖷 Send a fax to 44 (0) 1865 314091
🖳 Visit the Heinemann bookshop at www.heinemann.co.uk/library to browse our catalogue and order online.

First published in Great Britain by Heinemann Library, Halley Court, Jordan Hill, Oxford OX2 8EJ, part of Harcourt Education.
Heinemann is a registered trademark of Harcourt Education Ltd.

Editorial: Clare Lewis
Design: Victoria Bevan, Michelle Lisseter, and Bridge Creative Services
Illustrations: Stephen Lings and Jane Pickering at Linden Artists
Picture Research: Hannah Taylor
Production: Helen McCreath

Printed and bound in China by WKT

10 digit ISBN 0 431 05655 2
13 digit ISBN 978 0 431 05655 5

10 09 08 07 06
10 9 8 7 6 5 4 3 2 1

British Library Cataloguing in Publication Data
Theodorou, Rod and Telford, Carole
Amazing journeys: Down a river – 2nd edition
577.6'4
A full catalogue record for this book is available from the British Library.

Acknowledgements
The publishers would like to thank the following for permission to reproduce photographs:
Bruce Coleman Limited pp. **13** (top), **23** (bottom; EPL (Rob Visser); Buddy Mays pp. **10**, **11** (bottom), **13** (bottom), **15** (top and bottom), **26**; Corbis/Andrew Holbrooke p. **27**; Corbis Royalty Free p. **20**; NHPA (Daniel Heinclin) p. **23** (bottom); Oxford Scientific Films (Nick Bergkessee) p. **17** (top), (Alan and Sandy Carey) p. **21** (middle), (Daniel J. Cox) p. **11** (top), (Jack Dermid) p. **19** (top), (Pat and Tom Leeson) p. **21** (top), (Zig Leszczynski) p. **21** (bottom), (Joe McDonald) p. **19** (bottom), (E. Robinson) p. **25** (top); Rainbow (Dan McCoy) pp. **16**, **17** (bottom).
Opposite: Magnum Photos.

Cover photograph of a smallmouth bass, reproduced with permission of Still Pictures/Lynn Rogers.

Every effort has been made to contact copyright holders of any material reproduced in this book. Any omissions will be rectified in subsequent printings if notice is given to the publishers.

The paper used to print this book comes from sustainable resources.

Contents

Some words are shown in bold letters, **like this.**
You can find out what these words mean by
looking in the Glossary.

Introduction

You are about to go on an amazing journey.
We are going to travel along the mighty
Missouri-Mississippi River, the largest river in
the United States. You will start at the source of
the Missouri in the Rocky Mountains and travel
hundreds of kilometres past grasslands, until you
meet the Mississippi River. You will continue
travelling south, through **marsh** and **swamp**,
until we reach the sea.

On the way you will see an amazing variety of
birdlife and many other different kinds of plants
and animals. You will also learn about the life of
a major river – how rivers begin and end, and how
important they are for the health of the world.

The US writer Mark Twain
called the Mississippi
"the crookedest river
in the world".

Rivers always start on high ground and flow downwards towards a lake or the sea. The Missouri-Mississippi follows this same pattern. Like many rivers its life is often compared to the life of a person. It spends its childhood rushing down high ground at speed, tumbling over rocks and waterfalls. When it is grown up it winds its way gently through valleys. Then it reaches old age, where it slows down until it finally ends its life at the sea.

The Missouri - Mississippi network forms the fourth largest river in the world.

KEY

MISSISSIPPI RIVER

MISSOURI RIVER

Journey map

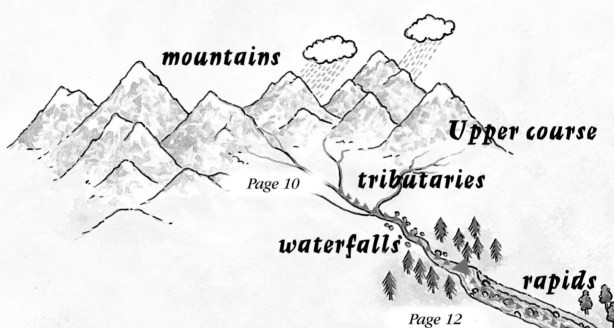

mountains

Upper course

tributaries

Page 10

waterfalls

rapids

Page 12

Page 14

This map shows the three different sections of the river. Each section has a name. The upper course is the young river. The middle course is the grown-up river, which winds its way along slowly like a giant snake. The lower course is the old river, where it divides into many smaller slower rivers, and meets the sea.

Page 16

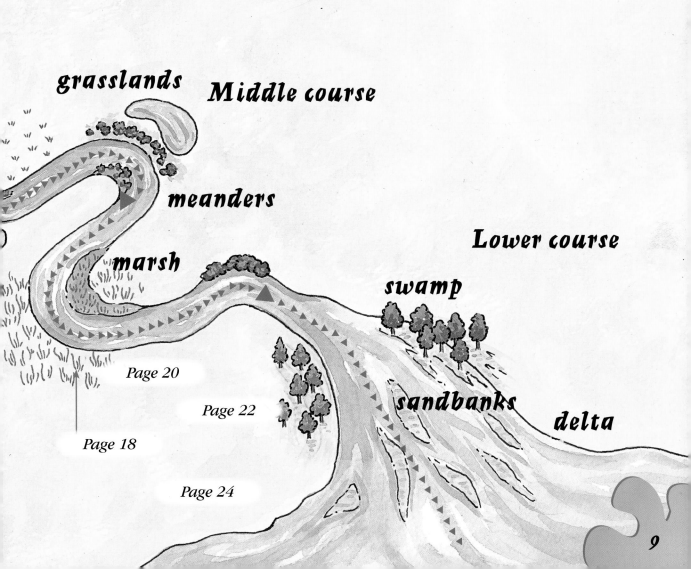

grasslands

Middle course

meanders

Lower course

marsh

swamp

Page 20

Page 22

sandbanks

delta

Page 18

Page 24

Birth of a river

We are standing in the Rocky Mountains in the middle of a pine forest. The air is fresh but very cold. It has just stopped raining. We can hear the sound of rushing water nearby . We walk carefully over mossy rocks until we reach a fast-moving stream. The water is rushing down the high mountain, tumbling over rocks and **boulders**.

Below we can see where this stream meets other streams, called tributaries. Rain falls on the mountains, forming hundreds of tributaries. These join together to form a river. This is where the Missouri River starts. It is called its source.

This small tributary helps form the huge Missouri River.

Black bear

This huge bear will eat almost anything. The black bear spends the winter in a deep sleep beneath a fallen tree or inside a cave at the source of the river.

Waterfalls

As the water flows over rocks it cuts into them. Over thousands of years it cuts deeper and deeper into the hillside, forming a V-shaped valley.

In very steep places the fast water cuts into soft rocks, but cannot wear away hard rock. This forms steps in the rocks. The river tumbles down these steps in waterfalls.

soft rock

hard rock

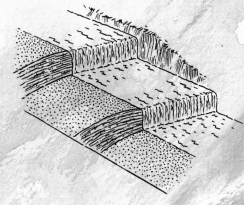

Into the rapids

One of the most exciting ways to travel down this part of the river is in a **canoe**. We grip onto our paddles, pushing them into the water to keep our balance. We have to be very careful. The fast-flowing river is wild and powerful. It rushes through **canyons**, past white cliffs, swirling around hard rocks. Sometimes it rushes over hundreds of **boulders** and small waterfalls. These are called rapids. The noise is deafening. We get soaked by the white foaming water.

You would need a canoe or raft to travel through these rapids.

Rainbow trout

These fish are powerful and **streamlined** to survive in the fast-flowing water. Rainbow trout swim **upriver**, sometimes leaping up over the rapids and waterfalls.

Moose

In the summer this giant deer likes to enter shallow water to eat water plants and escape biting flies and **mosquitoes**. Moose are very good swimmers and can even dive underwater to find tasty plants.

Golden eagle

Here among the canyons, we are lucky enough to see one of these **rare** and magnificent hunters on its huge nest. The nest may be as wide as a car! These huge birds hunt rabbits, prairie dogs, and even small deer.

Along the valley

The river valley is much wider now. We travel past woods and **prairie** grasslands. With binoculars we can see a **prairie dog town**. Above the croaking frogs we hear the howls of distant coyotes.

osprey

prairie falcon

great horned owl

prairie dogs

beaver

white-tailed deer

raccoon

wild turkey

bull snake

rock wrens

river otters

salamander

Beaver

The beaver is the biggest rodent in the United States. Beavers cut down small trees by **gnawing** them with their huge teeth. They use these logs and other sticks and mud to make huge **dams** across the river. By damming parts of the river the beavers make ponds where they can live and build their homes, called lodges.

River otters

It is hard to catch sight of these shy animals. Sometimes a family of river otters can be seen playing on the riverbank or sliding down mudbanks. Otters sometimes stand up on their two back legs to sniff the air for **predators**.

Prairie dogs

These animals live in hundreds of burrows called a town. Some of the prairie dogs act as "look-outs", watching for enemies such as coyotes, eagles, or foxes. This dog is giving the "all-clear" signal, telling the others a predator has moved on.

Magnificent meanders

We have now entered the middle course of the river. The valley is flat so the river **current** has slowed down, but it is still powerful. Instead of cutting downwards into the rock it cuts sideways into the bank. This makes the river twist from side to side in huge bends called meanders. Soil from the banks enters the river, making it muddy and full of rich **nutrients**. This helps more water plants grow which feed even more animal life. We see herons, some standing very still, some **wading** by the shallow banks.

Both the Missouri and the Mississippi have amazing meanders.

Ruby-throated hummingbird

This tiny bird flaps its wings so fast they make a humming sound. Hummingbirds can **hover** and even fly backwards. Their tiny nests are as small as egg-cups.

Great blue heron

The largest bird in the United States, the great blue heron, measures 2 metres (6.5 feet) across its wings! It wades through the water on its long legs, looking for fish and frogs which it spears with its long beak.

Making meanders

As the river swings around a bend it slices into the far side of the bank, cutting away the soil. While it is cutting one side of the bank, it dumps sand and stone by the other bank. This makes the bend bigger and bigger.

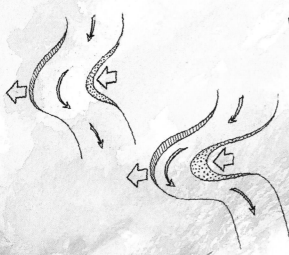

Marshlands

Further down the valley the land is even flatter. In some parts the river has no real banks at all. Water has spread into the surrounding area to form **wetlands**. When lots of reeds and rushes grow over this wetland it forms a **marsh**. Marshes are wonderful places for birds to hide and nest in.

yellow-headed blackbird

northern harrier

damselfly

bittern

reeds

muskrat

meadow vole

ruddy duck

marsh wren

garter snake

painted turtle

Mudpuppy

A mudpuppy is a large salamander that likes muddy or weedy waters. It eats crayfish, worms, snails, and other **aquatic** insects.

Bullfrog

The bullfrog is the largest North American frog. It feeds on tadpoles, crayfish, salamanders, worms, and even mice or ducklings.

Muskrat

The muskrat looks like a huge rat with a large flat tail which it uses as a **rudder** to help it swim. If attacked, muskrats show off their big teeth or hide under water. They can hold their breath for up to 12 minutes.

The flood plain

The Missouri has at last met the mighty Mississippi. We take a ride on a **tug** heading south **downriver**. Much of this part of the river is channelled by stone walls, earth banks, and huge **dams**. We see other tugs pushing long columns of barges. We pass steelworks and other factories, as well as towns and cities.

The flat land around us is called the flood plain. If there is a year of heavy rains the river may burst its banks. Then all the towns, cities, and farmlands here may be in danger. The dams and wooded shorelines are not as wild as before, but they are still home to nesting birds. We catch sight of a pair of bald eagles circling overhead.

A dam on the Mississippi, built to control the height of the river to make it safer for ships to use.

Bald eagle

Bald eagles spend the winter near dams. Their heads are not bald but are covered in white feathers. They can live for up to 50 years. They hunt small mammals, other birds, and fish.

Canada goose

Huge flocks of these large geese fly up the Missouri-Mississippi to spend the summer in Canada. Sometimes we see them with their young geese, called goslings.

Cottonmouth snake

The cottonmouth snake is **venomous** and may reach 1.5 metres (5 feet) in length. Its mouth is as white as cotton inside – but you only see this when it bites!

Into the swamp

We are now in the hot deep south of the country. Around us are huge **swamps**. These **wetlands** are home to many unusual animals. We see turtles, terrapins, and snakes sunning themselves on logs. Then we see a log which moves! It's an alligator – the largest **reptile** in the United States!

Cypress trees

Spanish moss

hummingbird

blue heron

egret

alligator

terrapins

Alligator snapping turtle

The alligator snapping turtle stays underwater at the bottom of the swamp with its mouth wide open. On its tongue it has a small piece of red flesh that looks like a worm. When fish swim up to eat the "worm" it snaps them up with its powerful beak.

Alligator

Alligators are silent and very hard to spot in the still swamp waters. They grow up to 5 metres (16.5 feet) long and eat fish, turtles, and birds.

Crayfish

These small **crustaceans** fill the muddy water of the swamps and **bayous**. Crayfish are about as long as your hand. They are sometimes called mud-bugs.

At the delta

We are at the end of our journey. The old river has slowed so much it stops cutting into the banks and instead drops all the **silt** and mud it has carried along. These form **mudflats** and **sandbanks**. The river flows around these in hundreds of smaller channels, forming a huge delta. **Tidal** salty sea water washes up the delta. Worms and small **crustaceans** live in this salty mud, providing food for many shorebirds. They **wade** in the water and walk along the mudflats digging for food with their pointed beaks.

The Mississippi "bird's foot" delta is one of the largest in the world.

Sandpiper

This busy little shorebird runs quickly, just ahead of the slow, lapping waves, probing for small animals. Sandpipers are often seen in large groups called flocks.

Great egret

The great egret is a large, beautiful, white bird with a **crest** on its head. It stands very still in shallow water, watching for small fish. Then it darts its beak forward into the water like a spear to catch them.

Brown pelican

The brown pelican is a huge bird with a large bag or "pouch" beneath its beak. It flies above the sea, looking for fish, then it dives straight down. Just as it crashes into the water it shoots its head and beak forwards, catching the surprised fish in its pouch.

Conservation and the future

A river under threat

Along our journey we have seen hundreds of wonderful animals and plants. We have also seen how people use the river. We have seen massive factories that use up huge amounts of water. We have seen the **dams** and banks built to control the river and stop flooding. By stopping the **annual** floods many of the **wetlands** along the river have been drained and destroyed. The water in the river has also been **polluted** by factories and with **chemicals** used by farmers. This pollution kills many plants and animals.

Mississippi meanders have been straightened to make journeys quicker for **tugs** and barges.

Why are rivers and wetlands important?

Only now are people realizing how careful we must be not to damage wetlands and rivers. Without **marshes** and **swamps** many plants and animals may disappear for ever. Without lots of meanders and **sandbanks** to slow the water down, floods can be bigger and even more dangerous. In 1993 there was one of the worst floods ever. Whole cities were flooded and people and animals drowned.

The rivers we have travelled on flow through the heart of the United States. Like other great rivers they act like the **blood vessels** in our bodies. They carry the water that all living things need to live. If we damage and pollute them, we damage ourselves.

The Mississippi flood of 1993 caused £8 billion ($10 billion) in damage!

Glossary

annual	happens once a year
aquatic	lives in water
bayou	marshy area near a river
blood vessel	tube carrying blood around the body
boulder	huge rocks
canoe	narrow boat
canyon	deep channel through rock
chemicals	substances which can be mixed together to make new substances
crest	tuft of feathers sticking up on the head
crustacean	type of animal that has a hard shell (e.g. crab)
current	flow of the river
dam	wall blocking the flow of the river
downriver	towards the sea
gnaw	grind away with the teeth
hover	stay still in the air by flapping the wings very fast
marsh	land that is always wet
mosquito	tiny flying insect, which sometimes sucks blood
mudflat	muddy land sometimes covered with water
nutrient	substance taken in by plants and animals to help them grow

pollute	to poison, usually by chemicals
prairie	flat, grass-covered land
prairie dog town	network of homes (burrows) where prairie dogs live
predator	animal which hunts and eats other animals
rare	not many left, hard to find
reptile	cold-blooded animals covered in scales (e.g. snake)
rudder	used for steering a boat
sandbank	wall of sand
silt	tiny pieces of rock and mud which settle at the bottom of a river
streamlined	shaped to move through air or water easily
swamp	land that is covered by shallow water with trees and plants
tidal	the rise and fall of the surface of the sea
tug	boat used to pull bigger boats
upriver	towards the start of the river
venomous	having a poisonous bite
wade	walk through water
wetlands	marshy land

Find out more

Further reading

Biomes Atlases: Rivers and Lakes, Richard Beatty (Raintree, 2003)

Earth Files: Rivers and Lakes, Chris Oxlade (Heinemann Library, 2003)

The World's Top Ten: Rivers, Neil Morris (Chrysalis, 2003)

Wild Habitats: Rivers and Waterways, Louise and Richard Spilsbury (Heinemann Library, 2004)

Organizations

Birdlife International
Wellbrook Court
Girton Road
Cambridge
CB3 0NA
www.birdlife.net

Friends of the Earth
26-28 Underwood Street
London
N1 2PN
www.foe.co.uk

Using the Internet

If you want to find out more about rivers, you can go to one of the website addresses below. Alternatively, you can use a search engine, such as www.yahooligans.com or www.internet4kids.com, and type in a keyword such as "river", or a related subject such as "river pollution".

Websites

www.rspb.org.uk/youth/index.asp

This part of the RSPB website is devoted to young bird lovers, with activities and games as well as useful information.

library.thinkquest.org/28022/

This site, called "All Along a River", is written entirely by students.

Index